Always
Matt

Always Matt

A TRIBUTE TO MATTHEW SHEPARD

By **LESLÉA NEWMAN**

Foreword by **JASON COLLINS**

Illustrated by **BRIAN BRITIGAN**

Abrams ComicArts • New York

Editor: Howard W. Reeves
Design Manager: Pamela Notarantonio
Designer: Josh Johnson
Managing Editor: Marie Oishi
Production Manager: Alison Gervais

Library of Congress Control Number 2022952137

ISBN 978-1-4197-5942-0

The illustrations for this book were
drawn and colored digitally.

Printed and bound in China
10 9 8 7 6 5 4 3 2 1

Abrams ComicArts books are available at special discounts when purchased
in quantity for premiums and promotions as well as fundraising or educational
use. Special editions can also be created to specification. For details, contact
specialsales@abramsbooks.com or the address below.

Abrams ComicArts® is a registered trademark of Harry N. Abrams, Inc.

ABRAMS The Art of Books
195 Broadway, New York, NY 10007
abramsbooks.com

For Judy, Dennis, and Logan Shepard

and for Matt
may his memory always be for a blessing
—L.N.

To my family and partner, for being
there whether near or far
—B.B.

CONTENTS

FOREWORD

My name is Jason Collins and in 2014, I became the first out NBA basketball player to play in the league.

I never met Matthew Shepard, yet he is a big part of my coming-out story.

I was a nineteen-year-old sophomore at Stanford University the year Matt was killed simply because he was gay. I was almost exactly two years younger than Matt (my birthday is December 2, his is December 1). I was deeply closeted when I was in college. I knew I was gay, but I kept denying my feelings. I learned about Matt's murder from watching the news on a tiny thirteen-inch TV in my dorm room. Terrified, I retreated further into the closet. It took me fourteen years, until I was thirty-three years old, to say to another human being, "I am gay."

I came out privately in 2011, during the NBA lockout season, which meant there was a work stoppage. Without basketball to distract me, I was forced to ask myself, *Who do you want to be? What do you want out of life?* I wanted to be myself. So I came out, but only to a few close family members and friends.

In the summer of 2012, I was a free agent and signed with the Boston Celtics. I was asked to choose a number to wear on my jersey. I wanted my number to be significant to LGBTQ+ history, so I chose 98, to represent the year that Matthew Shepard was killed. Every time I wore my number 98 basketball jersey, I felt like I was giving a silent nod to the LGBTQ+ community, because I hadn't told anyone publicly why I chose that number. I was hiding in plain sight.

In February 2013, I was traded from the Boston Celtics to the Washington Wizards. Being traded is like starting a new job, and your teammates ask you the usual questions: "Where are you from?" "Are you married?" I was tired of telling lies.

I came out publicly in a *Sports Illustrated* article in May 2013. The reaction was overwhelmingly positive. One of the first people who called me was Judy Shepard, Matt's mother. She said, "Jason, just keep living your life. Don't feel you have to respond to every hater." She was being protective, just like a mom.

President Barack Obama also reached out to me. He told me my actions would make a positive impression on people I had never met. And that meant a lot to me, because as an athlete, and a gay Black man in America, my goal is to have a positive impact on people's lives.

In a similar fashion, *Always Matt: A Tribute to Matthew Shepard*

JASON
COLLINS

will have a positive influence on people whom the poet Lesléa Newman and the artist Brian Britigan have never met. Lesléa's text and Brian's illustrations encourage readers not to simply comprehend but to use their imaginations and truly experience the situation deeply and with great emotion.

I hope that *Always Matt* will be read by many people of all ages and in many schools. When I was young I never had a class in LGBTQ+ studies. I learned about Black history, about art history, and you know I learned about European history. I hope there are teachers brave enough to share this book with students. This is part of our history. This is American history. This is the truth. We must learn the truth and learn from the truth. We owe as much to Matt, who must never be forgotten.

—Jason Collins

PREFACE

Since October of 1998, I have told the story of Matthew Shepard's murder hundreds of times in almost all fifty states as I have traveled coast-to-coast speaking out against hate crimes and pleading for peace.

Matthew Shepard's murder was a watershed moment in the struggle for LGBTQ+ rights, and he has become a legend. But Matthew Shepard is more than a hate crime victim. He was a person: a handsome young gay man with thoughts and feelings, likes and dislikes, hopes and dreams. And while he will continue to be mourned by those who knew and loved him as well as those who never had the chance to meet him, now that more than a quarter of a century has passed, I decided to tell the story in a different way: a way that celebrates and pays tribute to Matt and the short life that he lived.

I chose to speak about Matt in verse because poetry is the best way I know to get to the heart of the matter. It also leaves a great deal of empty space on the page, which mirrors the empty space Matt left behind when he was taken from this world. As the book developed, I realized there needed to be a way for that empty space to remain and be filled at the same time. Brian Britigan's haunting, sparse illustrations do exactly that.

Finally, hoping to inspire others to work for social justice and peace as Matt would have done, I concluded the book with a prose section that elevates the efforts of some of my heroes whose actions have made a difference, and to suggest ways to move forward and honor Matt's memory.

Reader, I invite you to turn the page and meet Matthew Shepard, known to his friends and family as Matt.

Always Matt

He was a grandson, a son, and a brother.
To the world, he was Matthew Shepard.
To his family, he was always Matt.

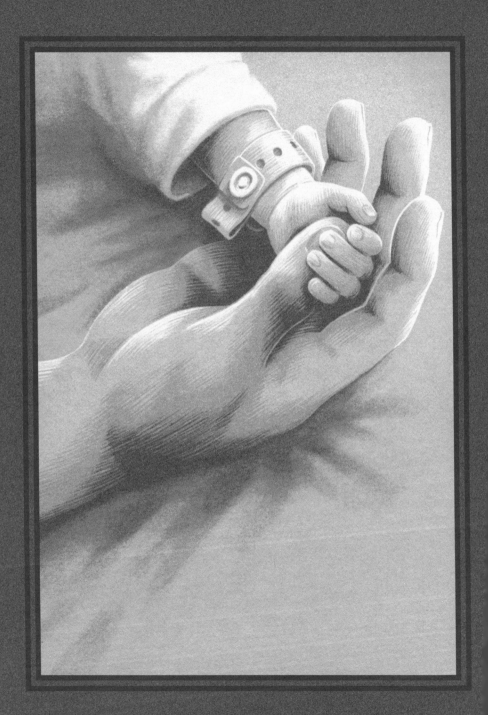

Matt was born with muddy blue eyes
and blond peach-fuzz hair
on a windy Wyoming December day.

He loved cuddling his stuffed rabbit, Oscar, and reading *Where the Wild Things Are* and singing "Twinkle, Twinkle, Little Star."

He loved wearing his dad's cowboy hats
and his mom's curlers
and dressing up as Dolly Parton for Halloween.

He loved leaving poems and drawings
and pretty rocks
in the mailboxes of his neighbors.

He loved hiking and fishing and horseback riding
and gazing through his telescope
at the sparkling stars in the wide Wyoming sky.

Matt loved his mother and father and brother most of all. Someday he hoped to fall in love with a man and start a family of his own.

He loved listening to people tell stories
about their lives. He heard happy stories
and sad stories. He listened very carefully.

He promised to make the world
a better place, a kinder place,
a peaceful place for everyone.

Matt went to college and made many friends,
all types of friends. Some of them
were gay and out and proud. Like him.

One windy Wyoming October night,
Matt met two men.
He was happy to talk to them.

He was always happy to make new friends.
Matt loved people.
But these two men didn't love Matt.

Their hearts were hard
and they hated Matt
because he was gay.

They drove Matt outside of town
and after they hurt him
and tied his hands to a buck rail fence

they left him alone, bruised and bleeding
under the wide Wyoming sky.
The moon and stars watched over him.

The smell of pine and sagebrush
kept him company.
A deer curled up close by.

The sun rose high in the sky.
And when evening arrived
a mountain biker found Matt.

Matt slept in a hospital bed.
Nurses and doctors cared for him.
His mother and father sat beside him.

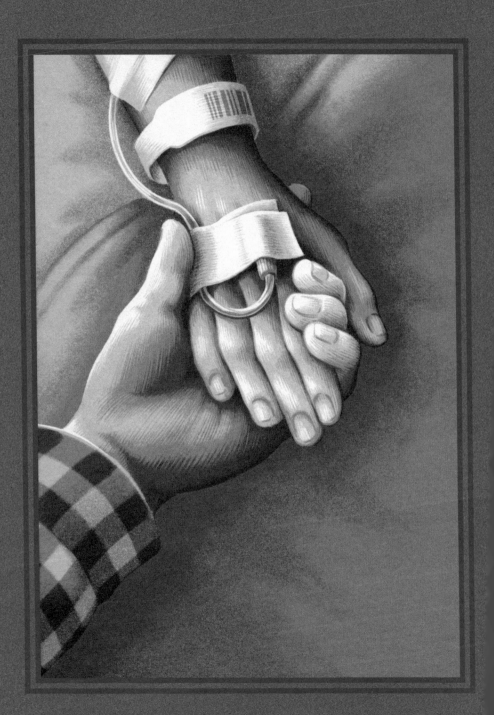

They played his favorite music.
They stroked his hands and face.
His brother whispered into his ear.

People heard what happened to Matt.
They gathered all over the world.
They held hands. They lit candles. They prayed.

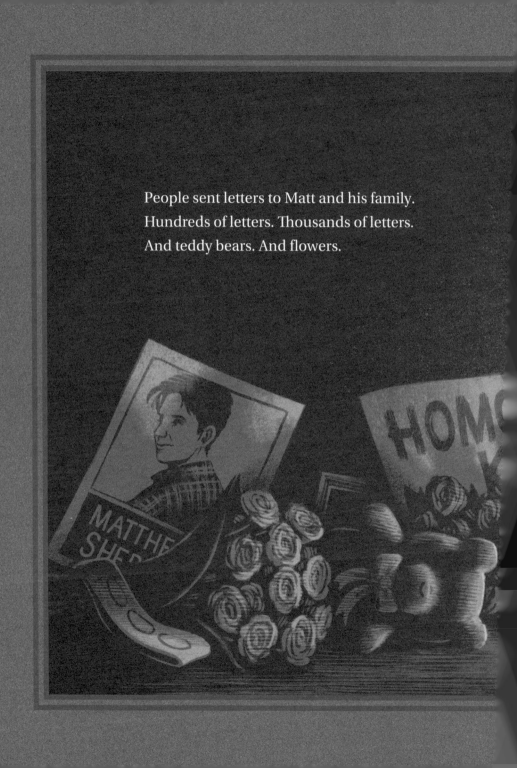

People sent letters to Matt and his family.
Hundreds of letters. Thousands of letters.
And teddy bears. And flowers.

So many people sent words of love.
But all the love in the world
couldn't keep Matt alive.

On the day of Matt's funeral,
a cold wind blew and a heavy snow
fell from the wide Wyoming sky.

Matt's friends flew in from all over the world.
The church filled quickly. People huddled outside
in the cold and snow and sang "Amazing Grace."

Matt's family received more letters.
Hundreds of letters. Thousands of letters.
People were sad. People were angry.

People wanted to do something.
Matt's family wanted to do something.
What would Matt do?

Matt promised to make the world
a better place, a kinder place,
a peaceful place for everyone.

Matt wanted to make a difference.
Now Matt's mom and dad make a difference.
They travel all over the world

to tell people Matt's story.
They talk about Matt, who was smart
and funny and friendly and kind.

They talk about Matt, who played
Abe Lincoln on History Day
and loved mac and cheese and Clayton the cat.

They talk about Matt,
hoping that people will soften their hearts
and accept everyone just as they are.

Millions of people have heard Matt's story
and are making a difference. They are writing
letters, marching, protesting, voting, passing laws.

They are doing their best to make
the world a better place, a kinder place,
a peaceful place for everyone.

He was a grandson, a son, and a brother.
To the world, he is Matthew Shepard.
To his family, he will always be Matt.

EPILOGUE

Because of Matthew Shepard, I have met thousands of people. But I never met Matt.

I missed him by one day.

In the spring of 1998, I received an invitation to fly out to Laramie and visit Matt's school, the University of Wyoming, to give the keynote speech for Gay Awareness Week, which was to take place a few months later in October. I was eager to talk to the students about my children's book *Heather Has Two Mommies*. Originally published in 1989, the book tells the story of a little girl named Heather who has two lesbian mothers, Mama Jane and Mama Kate. When Heather goes to school for the first time, she finds out that some people see her family as "different." When her teacher asks all the children in Heather's class to draw pictures of their families, Heather, her classmates, and readers of the book discover that there are all types of families and "the most important thing about a family is that all the people in it love each other."

A few days before my visit, Jim Osborn, the head of the University of Wyoming's Lesbian, Gay, Bisexual, Transgender Association, called to tell me that his friend Matt, also a member of the LGBT group, had been kidnapped, robbed, beaten, tied to a fence, and abandoned on the outskirts of town. He was found eighteen hours later by a mountain biker named Aaron Kreifels, who initially thought Matt was a scarecrow, possibly put up

JIM OSBORN

for Halloween. Matt was immediately taken to a hospital in Laramie and then transported to a larger hospital in Fort Collins, Colorado, that was better equipped to deal with his severe head injuries. No one knew whether he would live or die. By the time I received Jim Osborn's phone call, Matt's family, who were living outside the country at the time, had arrived at his bedside. The two local men who had attacked him had been arrested and were in jail. Needless to say, the university and the town were in an uproar. Given all that, Jim asked whether I was still willing to come.

"Yes," I said, without hesitation. "Gay Awareness Week must go on."

When I boarded my flight on Monday, October 12, I did not yet know that Matt had died early that morning, shortly after midnight. I found out

LESLÉA
NEWMAN

from the young woman who picked me up at the airport in Denver, Colorado, and drove me three hours to the University of Wyoming campus. There, I met Jim Osborn, a big, burly sweetheart of a man, who hugged me tightly as I fell weeping into his arms.

A few hours later, I stood onstage, ready to give the speech I had prepared, which focused on respect, acceptance, and celebration of all types of people and families. I looked down at the front row, which was filled with the students of the LGBT Association. They gazed up at me with faces full of hope, fear, and sorrow. They had left one empty seat right in the middle of the row. *Matt's seat*, I thought, and quickly swallowed the lump in my throat so I could go on with my presentation.

At the end of my talk, I promised Matt's friends and teachers that from that day forth I would work for LGBT rights as a way to honor Matt's memory. And for the past several decades, I have traveled around the country speaking out against hate.

And I am not alone.

December 1, 1998, would have been Matt's twenty-second birthday. He had planned on working hard to make the world a safer and more just place. He wanted to make a difference. To honor his memory, his parents, Judy and Dennis Shepard, created the Matthew Shepard Foundation, hoping to replace hate with understanding, compassion, and acceptance. Their mission is to "amplify the story of Matthew Shepard to inspire individuals, organizations, and communities to embrace the dignity and equality of all people." To this day, Matt's parents travel all over the world. By sharing their son's story and their experience as a family forever changed by a vicious hate crime, they transform hearts and minds and emphasize the importance of standing up for the LGBTQ+ community.

DENNIS &
JUDY SHEPARD

What happened to Matt should not happen to anyone. Two young men thought it was okay to lie to him and tell him that they were gay in order to befriend him and gain his trust. Two young men offered him a ride home, never intending to take him home at all. Two young men kidnapped, robbed, beat, and murdered Matt simply because he was gay. These two men, Russell Henderson and Aaron McKinney, are now in jail, each of them serving two consecutive life terms without any

GENE ROBINSON

chance of parole. They will remain imprisoned for the rest of their lives.

What happened to Matt's family should not happen to any family. They lost a beloved brother, son, and grandson. They endured antigay protestors brandishing signs of hate at Matt's funeral. They sat through a murder trial. They miss Matt every single day. As his parents said in a statement released on the morning of Matt's death, "He came into the world premature and left the world premature."

Matt's body was cremated, and for twenty years, his parents kept his remains in their home in a small oak chest decorated with a ceramic mountain scene, concerned that anywhere they buried him might be vandalized. Matt always loved the Episcopal Church, and on October 25, 2018, his ashes were interred in the Washington National Cathedral, which provides a final resting place for prominent Episcopalians. Bishop Gene Robinson, who in 2003 became the first openly gay priest to be elected bishop in the Episcopal Church, presided over a public Service of Thanksgiving and Remembrance, a celebration of Matt's life.

MOISÉS KAUFMAN

"Gently rest in this place," said Bishop Robinson. "You are safe now. Matt, welcome home."

Matt's parents find comfort in knowing that his ashes are interred in a house of prayer that welcomes everyone. In a public statement, Judy Shepard said, "It's reassuring to know he now will rest in a sacred spot where folks can come to reflect on creating a safer, kinder world."

Countless people have joined the fight to make the world a safer, kinder world in Matt's memory. While Matt lay in the hospital, many vigils took place. People around the country stood in silence, held candles, and prayed, demonstrating that it was possible for thousands of strangers to stand side by side in peace.

One month after Matt died, Moisés Kaufman, the founder and artistic director of the Tectonic Theater Project, along with nine members of the troupe, traveled from New York to Laramie. They interviewed many people who lived in town, asking them how Matt's murder affected them. These interviews became *The Laramie Project*, one of the most frequently performed plays in America. Audiences are encouraged to discuss the play and find ways to work together to erase hate in their own communities. A decade later, members of the Tectonic Theater Project returned to Laramie, conducted more interviews, and created *The Laramie Project—Ten Years Later: The Epilogue*, which shows that the effects of Matt's murder on Laramie, the state of Wyoming, the USA, and the entire world are far from over.

One year after Matt died, eleven people gathered to plan a counterprotest after hearing that members of the Westboro Baptist Church, the same group that had protested Matt's funeral, were going to show up at his murder trial. Dressed in white angel costumes with ten-foot wingspans, the eleven "angels" stood

silently with their backs turned to the protestors, blocking the homophobic signs they brandished in the air. Since this first demonstration, many similar Angel Actions have taken place, offering a message of peace and compassion to counteract messages of hate.

Ten years after Matt died, the University of Wyoming erected a bench in his memory. The bench is a peaceful place to sit and think about ways to make the world a better place. The plaque on the bench reads:

MATTHEW WAYNE SHEPARD
DECEMBER 1, 1976 - OCTOBER 12, 1998
BELOVED SON, BROTHER, AND FRIEND
HE CONTINUES TO MAKE A DIFFERENCE
PEACE BE WITH HIM AND ALL WHO SIT HERE

Many people who visit the University of Wyoming campus spend time on Matt's bench to remember him and to think about what they can do to prevent further horrific crimes from ever taking place.

Eleven years after Matt died, President Barack Obama signed into law a Hate Crimes Prevention Act. Along with Matt, the law is named for James Byrd Jr., an African American man who in 1998 was murdered in Jasper, Texas, by three white supremacists after accepting a ride home from them. The tireless work of many people, including Judy and Dennis Shepard, was instrumental in passing this law. It was first introduced in April 2001 and

BARACK
OBAMA

took five congressional sessions to get through. The Matthew Shepard and James Byrd Jr. Hate Crimes Prevention Act was signed into law on October 28, 2009, by President Obama. At the reception commemorating the enactment of this law, President Obama thanked all the activists and organizers who made this victory possible: "You know that we've come far on the journey towards a more perfect union . . . through this law, we will strengthen the protections against crimes based on the color of your skin, the faith in your heart, or the place of your birth. We will finally add federal protections against crimes based on gender, disability, gender identity, or sexual orientation . . . no one in America should ever be afraid to walk down the street holding the hands of the person they love." The Justice Department continues to use the Matthew Shepard and James Byrd Jr. Hate Crimes Prevention Act to indict people who commit these types of crimes.

MICHELE JOSUE

Fifteen years after Matt died, Michele Josue, a high school friend of Matt's, created a film called *Matt Shepard Is a Friend of Mine* to recapture the Matt whom she loved, and whom the world barely knew. The film portrays Matt as he really was, "a complex, sensitive, gay young man who worked hard to find peace and his place in the world." The film has been widely shown and has received many prestigious awards. It deeply touches people who are old enough to remember the day that Matt was killed as well as people who were not yet born when his life was cut short so tragically.

Many people continue to work for social justice in Matt's memory. Students create or join LGBTQ+ groups at their schools. Teachers include lessons on LGBTQ+ literature and history and other subjects in their classrooms. People of all ages wear buttons on their backpacks or clothing that show support for the LGBTQ+ community, attend LGBTQ+ Pride marches and rallies, and write letters in support of LGBTQ+ rights to their local newspapers and representatives. They speak out when they hear someone make an antigay remark or commit a homophobic act. Most importantly, they reach out to members of the LGBTQ+ community to show them they are not alone.

©1998 Gina van Hoof/SOFAM

What can you do in Matt's memory in order to make a difference?

NOTES

AUTHOR

On October 12, 1998, when I headed for the airport en route to Laramie, to give the University of Wyoming's Gay Awareness Week's keynote speech, I knew I was starting out on a trip, but I didn't know I was also embarking on what has become a lifelong mission: to make the world a better place for LGBTQ+ youth. Matt's voice was forever silenced on that day; it is my responsibility, as well as my privilege to speak out as a way to honor his memory.

Change does happen, often one heart at a time. Once, after I gave a reading from my book *October Mourning: A Song for Matthew Shepard* at a Massachusetts high school, a member of the football team was so moved by Matt's story that he stood up in the auditorium and said in front of three hundred of his classmates, "I am never going to use the word 'gay' as an insult again." Another time, after I gave the same presentation at a college in Kentucky, a student ran out of the auditorium, threw open the door to a convenience store across the street, and strode over to the clerk behind the counter. "I just heard the story of Matthew Shepard," he said. "I'm sorry for teasing you about being gay. I promise not to do it anymore." Then he leaned across the counter and the two men embraced.

These experiences give me hope, courage, and the strength to keep speaking out on behalf of the LGBTQ+ community. It is easy to sink into despair; far too many hate crimes are committed every year and far too many lives are lost. Each and every one of us can—and must—make a difference. One doesn't have to do something enormous; often the smallest act makes the largest difference. As Jackie Chan said, "Sometimes it only takes one act of kindness and caring to change a person's life." And as the Buddha said, "When words are both true and kind, they can change the world."

I wrote *Always Matt* in hopes that each reader, after finishing the book, will be inspired to change the world by working for social justice and peace. Together, we can create the world that we want to live in: a world in which each of us is respected, accepted, and celebrated. A world that is safe for us all.

ARTIST

I can remember a string of high-profile news stories from my childhood, overheard on the car radio or an evening newscast: Oklahoma City, Bosnia, Columbine. But the reports of what happened in Laramie caught my ten-year-old ears differently. I recognized something within myself reflected in those words, transforming them into a cautionary tale that lurked in the back of my young mind. *These are the stakes. This is what could happen to you.*

My first task in illustrating this book was to re-examine the version of this story that I've held within myself for all these years. Guided by Lesléa's words, I began replacing my incomplete picture of Matthew Shepard, cobbled together from half-remembered broadcasts and faded newspaper articles, with one built from the memories of those who knew him simply as Matt. Creating these images became an attempt to fill the gaps in my own understanding, holding up my flawed assumptions to the light and replacing them with stark truths. My hope is that this book can be an invitation for others to do the same.

I can still see myself reflected in Matt's story, but my old fears have been replaced by new parallels. Like Matt, I came out to my family shortly before moving out west for college, built connections with other queer folks, and found confidence in the parts of myself I had purposefully hidden away. But I was lucky; I got to grow up in a world that had been changed for the better through the efforts of those touched by Matt's life and story. While the darkness at the center of this book can never be erased, I'm thankful for the opportunity to play a small part in amplifying the light that Judy, Dennis, Lesléa, and countless others have worked so hard to kindle.

AUTHOR'S RESOURCE LIST

BOOKS

Kaufman, Moisés, and the Members of the Tectonic Theater Project. *The Laramie Project*. New York: Vintage Books, 2001.

Kaufman, Moisés, Leigh Fondakowski, Greg Pierotti, Andy Paris, and Stephen Belber. *The Laramie Project and The Laramie Project: Ten Years Later*. New York: Vintage, 2014.

Loffreda, Beth. *Losing Matthew Shepard: Life and Politics in the Aftermath of Anti-Gay Murder*. New York: Columbia University Press, 2000.

Newman, Lesléa. *October Mourning: A Song for Matthew Shepard*. Somerville, MA: Candlewick Press, 2014.

Shepard, Judy. *The Meaning of Matthew: My Son's Murder in Laramie, and a World Transformed*. New York: Hudson Street Press, 2009.

FILMS

Josue, Michele. *Matt Shepard Is a Friend of Mine*. Virgil Films, 2015.

The Laramie Project. HBO Studios, 2002.

Seckinger, Beverly. *Laramie Inside Out*. 2004.

CD

Johnson, Craig Hella. *Considering Matthew Shepard*. Produced by Harmonia Mundi, 2016.

WEBSITES

The Matthew Shepard Foundation
matthewshepard.org

Matthew's Place
medium.com/matthews-place

The Trevor Project
thetrevorproject.org

It Gets Better
itgetsbetter.org

GLSEN (Gay, Lesbian, and Straight Educational Network)
glsen.org

PFLAG
pflag.org

GSA (Genders & Sexualities Alliance) Network
gsanetwork.org

Campus Pride
campuspride.org

ACKNOWLEDGMENTS

AUTHOR

My deepest, heartfelt appreciation goes to:

Judy and Dennis Shepard, the kindest people I know, for allowing me to tell their son's story;

Jim Osborn and the other members of the University of Wyoming's 1998 LGBT Association for inviting me to be their Gay Awareness Week Keynote Speaker and changing my life forever;

Cathy Renna, whom I met in Laramie in 1998 and whose work for LGBTQ+ rights has inspired me ever since;

Plynn Gutman, who traveled with me to Laramie in 2010 so I could once more stand beneath the wide Wyoming sky;

Aaron Hamburger, for his generous hospitality and for accompanying me to the Service of Thanksgiving and Remembrance honoring Matt at the Washington National Cathedral in 2018;

Jason Marsden, former Executive Director of the Matthew Shepard Foundation, who first suggested many years ago that I write this book;

Rob Sanders, my Long Time Friend, who read a very rough first draft of this manuscript and said, "Think of it as a poem," which made all the difference;

Elizabeth Harding, my infinitely patient, wise, and kind agent, who has advised me, supported me, and encouraged me for more than twenty years, as well as her assistants, Sarah Gerton and Jazmia Young;

Howard Reeves, my brilliant editor, who was enthusiastic, passionate, and totally committed to this project from the moment it landed on his desk;

Sara Sproull, Assistant Editor Extraordinaire, who always answers my endless queries in rapid time and with great cheer;

Jason Collins, for his moving, poignant, and inspiring foreword to *Always Matt*, and for everything he does to make the world a safer place for the LGBTQ+ community;

Gina van Hoof, whose beautiful photograph of Matt takes my breath away every time I look into his eyes;

Brian Britigan, the talented and amazing artist whose incredible illustrations brought my words to life so beautifully they made me cry;

Craig Hella Johnson, whose breathtaking music, including the fusion oratorio *Considering Matthew Shepard*, has healed my heart and the hearts of so many;

My friends, colleagues, and family members who have been there for me—too many to mention, but if you think you are part of this pack, you are;

And finally, Mary Grace Newman Vazquez, whose steadfast love is my home.

ARTIST

I owe a debt of gratitude to those who have kept Matt's story alive with compassion and creativity; their efforts have been a guiding light for this project:

BRIAN BRITIGAN

To Judy Shepard, whose incredible openness in her writing and narration of *The Meaning of Matthew* became my north star while navigating the making of these images.

To Michele Josue, whose portrait of a missing subject in *Matt Shepard Is a Friend of Mine* helped me imagine all the small moments needed to bring this book to life.

To Moisés Kaufman and the Tectonic Theater Project, whose

efforts in *The Laramie Project* and its follow-up helped me find my own place in this story.

And thank you to those whose impact on this project, whether large or small, cannot be ignored:

To Lesléa Newman, for trusting me with her words and for her generous encouragement.

To Howard Reeves, for his guidance from this book's conception to its completion.

To Eugenia Mello, Sam Kalda, and Chad W. Beckerman, for their advice at the very beginning of this project, and to David Leutert for telling me when it was finished.

To James McMullan, for showing me how to fold oneself into the shape of a book.

To Marshall Arisman and Carl Titolo, whose words of wisdom came floating back to me as I first pictured these pages.

And as always, to my partner, George, for his patience on the days when I wanted to do nothing but draw as well as on the days when I wanted to do anything but.

BIOGRAPHIES

AUTHOR

Lesléa Newman is the author of eighty books for readers of all ages, including the novel-in-verse *October Mourning: A Song for Matthew Shepard*, the short story collection *A Letter to Harvey Milk*, the dual memoir-in-verse *I Carry My Mother* and *I Wish My Father*, the picture books *Sparkle Boy* and *The Boy Who Cried Fabulous*, and the children's classic *Heather Has Two Mommies*. Her honors and literary awards include the Matthew Shepard Foundation Making a Difference Award, a National Endowment for the Arts poetry fellowship, two American Library Association Stonewall Book Award Honors, two National Jewish Book Awards, the Association of Jewish Libraries Sydney Taylor Body-of-Work Award, and the Massachusetts Book Award. From 2008 to 2010, she served as the poet laureate of Northampton, Massachusetts. Seven of her poems from *October Mourning: A Song for Matthew Shepard* are included in the libretto of *Considering Matthew Shepard*, a fusion oratorio composed by Craig Hella Johnson. Newman lives in Holyoke, Massachusetts. lesleanewman.com

ARTIST

Born and raised in Iowa City, Iowa, Brian Britigan studied art and animation at the University of Washington in Seattle before earning an MFA in illustration from the School of Visual Arts in New York City. His illustrations have appeared in print and online publications such as the *New York Times*, the *Star Tribune*, and the *Progressive*, and he has created animations for documentary projects, including the Emmy-nominated *The Office of Missing Children*. Britigan is an instructor and mentor at the Minneapolis College of Art and Design. He lives in Minneapolis, Minnesota. brianbritigan.com